Disney MOVIE MAGIC

A piano accompaniment book (HL00841181) is available for this collection

Disney characters and artwork © Disney Enterprises, Inc.

ISBN 978-0-7935-7842-9

HAL•LEONARD® CORPORATION
7777 W. BLUEMOUND RD. P.O. BOX 13819 MILWAUKEE, WI 53213

For all works contained herein:
Unauthorized copying, arranging, adapting, recording or public performance is an infringement of copyright.
Infringers are liable under the law.

Visit Hal Leonard Online at

OUT OF THIN AIR
from Walt Disney's ALADDIN AND THE KING OF THIEVES

Cello

Words and Music by
DAVID FRIEDMAN

© 1996 Walt Disney Music Company
International Copyright Secured   All Rights Reserved

CAN YOU FEEL THE LOVE TONIGHT

from Walt Disney Pictures' THE LION KING

Cello

Music by ELTON JOHN
Lyrics by TIM RICE

© 1994 Wonderland Music Company, Inc.
International Copyright Secured All Rights Reserved

CIRCLE OF LIFE
from Walt Disney Pictures' THE LION KING

Cello

Music by ELTON JOHN
Lyrics by TIM RICE

Moderately (with an African beat)

© 1994 Wonderland Music Company, Inc.
International Copyright Secured   All Rights Reserved

HAKUNA MATATA
from Walt Disney Pictures' THE LION KING

Music by ELTON JOHN
Lyrics by TIM RICE

Cello

© 1994 Wonderland Music Company, Inc.
International Copyright Secured   All Rights Reserved

I JUST CAN'T WAIT TO BE KING

from Walt Disney Pictures' THE LION KING

Cello

Music by ELTON JOHN
Lyrics by TIM RICE

© 1994 Wonderland Music Company, Inc.
International Copyright Secured   All Rights Reserved

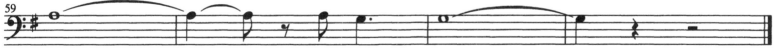

THIS LAND

from Walt Disney Pictures' THE LION KING

Cello

Music by
HANS ZIMMER

© 1994 Wonderland Music Company, Inc.
International Copyright Secured   All Rights Reserved

THE VIRGINIA COMPANY
from Walt Disney's POCAHONTAS

Music by ALAN MENKEN
Lyrics by STEPHEN SCHWARTZ

Cello

© 1995 Wonderland Music Company, Inc. and Walt Disney Music Company
International Copyright Secured   All Rights Reserved

COLORS OF THE WIND

from Walt Disney's POCAHONTAS

Cello

Music by ALAN MENKEN
Lyrics by STEPHEN SCHWARTZ

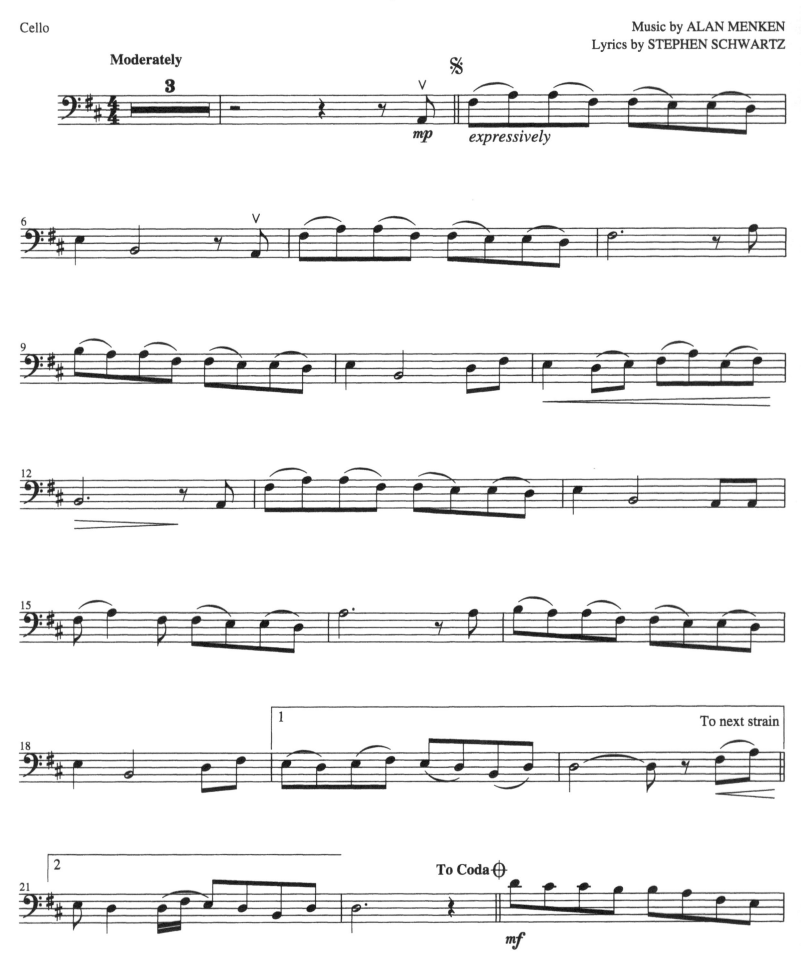

© 1995 Wonderland Music Company, Inc. and Walt Disney Music Company
International Copyright Secured   All Rights Reserved

mp

D.S. al Coda

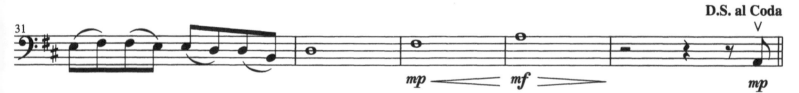

mp — < — mf — >   mp

✛ **CODA**

f — < — ff   mf

f

mf   mp

poco rall. < f mp   molto rall.

a tempo   p rall.

JUST AROUND THE RIVERBEND

from Walt Disney's POCAHONTAS

Music by ALAN MENKEN
Lyrics by STEPHEN SCHWARTZ

Cello

© 1995 Wonderland Music Company, Inc. and Walt Disney Music Company
International Copyright Secured   All Rights Reserved

MINE, MINE, MINE

from Walt Disney's POCAHONTAS

Cello

Music by ALAN MENKEN
Lyrics by STEPHEN SCHWARTZ

© 1995 Wonderland Music Company, Inc. and Walt Disney Music Company
International Copyright Secured   All Rights Reserved

CRUELLA DE VIL

from Walt Disney's 101 DALMATIANS

Words and Music by
MEL LEVEN

Cello

© 1959 Walt Disney Music Company
Copyright Renewed
International Copyright Secured   All Rights Reserved

FORGET ABOUT LOVE
from Walt Disney's THE RETURN OF JAFAR

Words and Music by
MICHAEL SILVERSHER and PATTY SILVERSHER

Cello

© 1994 Wonderland Music Company, Inc.
International Copyright Secured All Rights Reserved

Freely

a tempo

YOU'VE GOT A FRIEND IN ME

from Walt Disney's TOY STORY

Cello

Music and Lyrics by
RANDY NEWMAN

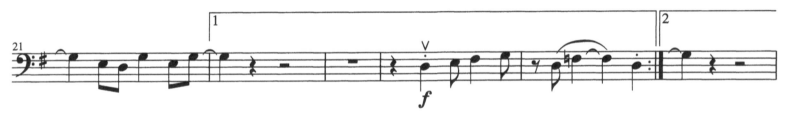

© 1995 Walt Disney Music Company
International Copyright Secured   All Rights Reserved

STRANGE THINGS

from Walt Disney's TOY STORY

Cello

Music and Lyrics by
RANDY NEWMAN

© 1995 Walt Disney Music Company
International Copyright Secured   All Rights Reserved